LIFE

Experience

Leading to Hell and Back to God

RONALD DEVERA

Fulton Books
Meadville, PA

Published by Fulton Books 2024

ISBN 979-8-88982-353-7 (paperback)
ISBN 979-8-88982-354-4 (digital)

Printed in the United States of America

To the Lincoln family, Devera family, and my friends Dan, Alan, Gary, and David, who helped me become the man I am today. I love my family and friends for the times we spent together every year.

CONTENTS

INTRODUCTION

Hello, my name is Ronald Ellsworth Devera, and I am going to tell my story of how my sins have affected my life. My wife, Julia Valerievna Devera, will also tell you about her experience in relation to my afterlife experience.

I will tell you my life story, explain the sins committed throughout my life, and how my death leads to our redemption and forgiveness by God our Father in Heaven.

Childhood

From age seven to eleven, I knew God intimately. I felt his presence inside of me until my sinful nature took hold of me, and I no longer felt it. I was a good kid in school, followed the rules, and did what I was supposed to. However, I learned later in life that being a good person is not enough to get you into Heaven. Knowing Jesus, being baptized, and following him is the only way.

Between the ages of ten and twelve, I had a girlfriend who I was head over heels in love with. Her name was Renee. I used to visit her on a regular basis and eventually told her about the pull God had within me. The pull was a feeling of walking a path God wanted me to follow with love and joy, seeking redemption for myself and others. I remember telling her and my friends about God, and they laughed at me. I took it in stride at the time. I was seeing Renee for a couple of years on a regular basis. I still remember the first time we kissed. I also remember the time she called me and told me she had sex with her best friend's brother. I was hurt and extremely angry, so I went looking for the young man she slept with at his house. I found him and began to beat him so badly that I could have killed him if it wasn't for a friend of my sister's and another person who stopped me. I never saw Renee or her friends again. When I look back at this now, it's more obvious than ever that God was there watching over me.

My parents, Helen E. Lincoln and Ronald E. Lincoln, lived in Parma, Ohio, where I was also born on July 25. I had an average childhood up until my dad left when I was seven. My mom asked my aunts and uncle from Pennsylvania to come and stay with us to help with my two brothers and me. I enjoyed having my aunts and uncle visiting.

When I got older, I took care of my two brothers on my own and ensured we got to school, did homework, got back home safely, and were fed on time. My mom was working full-time as a school bus driver, and my dad left us because of his sins he committed. I grew up fast since I was the older brother. I had too.

My mom eventually met another man, Richard Devera, and remarried on June 17, 1974. With my mom's marriage, I got a sister, and we all moved into Richard's house. The house was cramped since it was meant for a family of three, and we now had a family of six. My brother and I shared a bedroom, my youngest brother got his own room, and my mom and dad slept in the basement. My older sister slept in the attic bedroom. Eventually, my mom and Richard bought a bigger house we all moved into, and unlike before, we all got our own rooms. It was a good period in my life when I got my own room and had many friends. Dan, Alan, Gary, Jim, and Joe were my closest and most trustworthy friends.

From age twelve to eighteen, there was a war inside of me between my sinful nature and my desire to be a good person, but not a godly person. What good there was in me from my family support was always fighting for me to be the type of individual I desired to be and do what was right. However, this was not what I needed. I needed to turn to God, but of course, I did not do this. My sinful nature got the best of me. My mom and grandma would always tell me to change my ways. I stopped believing in the church of God because I saw things the church was doing that were wrong based on my own understanding, such as ridiculing people on how they look instead of how they act and not living by what the Bible states. Jesus said we must be careful in the churches we attend as some churches will lead you astray because they are not of God. You can see these churches today by looking for whether or not their sermons align with the Bible and not the beliefs of society.

From age twelve to age forty-four, I would attend church on holidays only, usually Christmas and Easter, or with my grandma Daisy and other family members during the year. I did not read the Bible on my own, as we all should. In fact, my mom and grandma were the only reason I ever heard scripture word for word as they would read it to my brothers and me. God was trying to give me a wake-up call, and I was not listening. I went further down my sinful path.

By the time I reached age forty-four, I broke nine of the Ten Commandments as shown below. I truly lost my way and was heading away from God and toward satan's trap.

The Ten Commandments:

1. Thou shalt have no other gods before me.
2. Thou shalt not make unto thee any graven images.
3. Thou shalt not take the Lord's name in vain.
4. Remember the Sabbath Day to keep it holy.
5. Honor thy Father and Mother.
6. Thou shall not murder.
7. Thou shalt not commit adultery.
8. Thou shalt not steal.
9. Thou shall not bear false witness against your neighbor.
10. Thou shalt not covet thy neighbor's house, wife, or possessions.

C H A P T E R   2

Military

I worked at Antonio's Pizza Restaurant from ninth grade to twelfth grade. I graduated in January 1982 and went into the army as an infantryman. I didn't know how I was going to pay for college; therefore, I joined the military to get the college kicker that would help pay for university, help me grow up and learn about the world. I spent four years in the army, one year in Korea and three years at Fort Polk, Louisiana. I left the army as a specialist E-4 honorable discharge.

In Korea, I met a lot of beautiful women whom I became intimate with, and we had a lot of fun. I met this one woman at a bar who was celebrating her upcoming marriage. We drank a lot of soju and wine. We went to a hotel and made love to each other before she got married. I was her final fling before she got married.

At Fort Polk, Louisiana, I met a Korean woman whom I lived with who I wanted to marry. I called my dad to ask his advice on this woman who I thought I was in love with. He said, "Are you ready to settle down with her, be committed to her for the rest of your life?"

I didn't get married for we both were not ready for that commitment.

C H A P T E R   3

University

After the military, I went home and started to look into universities to attend so I could then go and find my career job. I found a job at British Petroleum (BP), a gas station in Parma, Ohio. I then found Kent State University, which had a good criminal justice program, so I applied and got in. I transferred my job at BP to the area near Kent, Ohio. I worked ten-hour shifts four days a week at night and went to school full-time during the day. My boss was great and would let me work Thursday through Sunday every week until I graduated. I finished university in three and a half years.

I went to the gym on a regular basis to keep in shape and practice karate. During university, I met this woman who became interested in me, and we had a fling until she met someone, and we went our separate ways as friends. While attending Kent State University, I would see this really pretty athletic girl on campus every once in a while. She came to my work one late night out of the blue since I worked in Streetsboro, and Kent State University was the next town over. Before I knew it, we were having sex. I was committing adultery, a sin since she was not my wife. I never talked to her again, except every once in a while I would see her on campus walking.

I read a lot of *Playboy* magazines and watched a lot of porn during my life from age eighteen to year 2008. I thought this was okay, but I learned later I was wrong. I threw all these items in the

5

trash in 2009, including anything connected to evil such as false gods, tarot cards, etc.

After graduating with my criminal justice degree, I had a hard time finding work, so I then went to the police academy at the University of Akron. I passed the police certification test for Ohio and started to look for work. I got the job at Coshocton County Department of Job and Family Services. I should have known something was wrong when they asked me if I really wanted the job. I worked there for three months, and they let me go. I found out later they hired my boss's daughter. They were giving preference to a coworker's daughter even though I had a better score on the test. I understood why this happened. Family is important.

Soon I moved back home, and my friend Alan called me about a federal job about a month later. It was a reminder that God was still watching over me.

C H A P T E R   4

Permanent Job

The next morning, I went downtown to the federal building to interview for a federal position in military retired payroll general service level (GS) 3. I would process military retirees' pay for the month using laws and regulations so they would get their pay on time without any errors. The interviewer called me the following day to accept the position as a GS-3. I accepted the job and started the following week. I had two weeks of training on military retired payroll. I loved this job and was good at it.

I soon attended Cuyahoga Community College (CCC) to get my associate degree in accounting. I worked my way up by doing extra duties and learning new jobs in retired payroll to a general service level GS6 lead retired payroll position. In this position, I would review the work of others to ensure it was processed properly using laws and regulations. If not done properly, I would send it back with notes for them to correct.

I applied for an accountant internship GS-7 to GS-11 in the federal government. I got the position in August 1999 and had to transfer to Columbus, Ohio. For three years, I spent this time moving to Columbus, Ohio, where I bought my first house, a two-bedroom ranch style with a two-and-a-half-car garage. I bought this house because it was ten minutes to my job located in Columbus, Ohio.

I went from GS-7 to a GS-11 and had many experiences doing accountant jobs throughout the federal government. I kept volunteering for different jobs, like a six-month tour at a military base in California doing accounting data analysis. I found I had a knack for it, and it was fun to find fraud issues. I returned to school to get my master's in business administration (MBA). Eventually, I'd be promoted to GS-12 auditor, and then I got my GS-13 lead auditor position. As the lead auditor, I reviewed the work of other auditors to ensure proper referencing to findings the auditors identified with laws and regulations.

C H A P T E R   5

Medical Issues

The following is all the medical issues I have. In 1984, while in the army during my time in Korea, I caught pneumonia for a week and recovered in the military's base hospital. In 1985, while working on an armored personnel carrier (APC), I got hurt while tightening a bolt when the tool slipped and hit my chin area. I went to the hospital for a minor injury, which gave me a cold sore on the corner of my mouth. In 1987 at age twenty-one, I had a gout attack on my left foot and saw my family doctor. Since then, I've had multiple gout attacks from that period on. In 1999, I learned I developed high cholesterol and high blood pressure, which I take medication for every day. In 2000, I had a heart attack that resulted in me having to go to the hospital. While admitted, I had to have surgery where two stents were put in my heart to open the blood vessels.

In 2001, I found out I had kidney stones, and my kidney function was at level 2. When kidneys stop functioning normally, your waste products build up in your body, which starts to harm other organs, and you feel tired and sick. In 2002, I had chest pains again and went into hospital for surgery; stents were inserted in my heart to open blood vessels. In 2004, I had chest pains again and went into hospital for surgery; additional stents were inserted in my heart. In 2006, I had chest pains again and went into hospital for surgery; more stents were inserted into my heart. For each of these stent sur-

9

geries, I had three months of recovery. In November 2008, I had chest pains and went back into hospital. On December 3, 2008, I had open-heart surgery. I died on the operating table and was revived by God, who heard prayers for my doctors and me from family, friends, and others. In December 13, 2008, I woke up from a ten-day coma. I became a born-again Christian. Doctors and nurses said I was a miracle for 2008.

On December 18, 2008, I was released from the hospital to recover. It took only a couple of months for me to recover from this open-heart surgery. In 2009, I was having problems walking without pain. I saw a specialist doctor who said I had hurt the bones in both sides of my feet. I had to wear special shoes or inserts to stop the issue. My bones would never return to their natural form.

But God had other plans for me as they did recover. In October 2011, I became very sick, and I could not understand why, so my regular doctor sent me to an oncologist. In December 2011, I discovered I had cancer, lymphoma. In January 2012, I got a CT scan to discover it was level 2 cancer. The CT scan also disclosed I had arthritis in my hands, elbows, and feet. I cried and felt very sad, then I laughed about it, but I gave this to God to take care of my cancer.

In April 2013, I was getting headaches all the time. On August 24, 2013, I had surgery on my brain to close off a dural arteriovenous shunt. In December 2014, headaches returned, which were different from before. The headaches eventually went away, and the noise in my ear went away. God was watching over me.

In November 2014, I suffered a major heart attack, taking my heart function down to 25 percent. I was tired all the time now. I requested disability retirement from Defense Finance and Accounting Service (DFAS), my job, in February 2015. On August 1, 2015, my disability retirement was approved. The wife and I reached out to Cleveland Clinic to see if I could have heart transplant. The Cleveland Clinic doctors recommended I wait five years since I just found out about my lymphoma.

On March 23, 2019, I was at stage 5 kidney failure, and my heart was having issues with water buildup around the heart, causing me to be more tired than before. Can you imagine where you are sleeping ten to eighteen hours a day? You are basically sleeping your life away. My doctor put me on medication to help remove excess water. My kidney and heart doctors recommended a transplant for both. In November 2018, the wife and I met with Cleveland Clinic heart and kidney transplant doctors. I had four days of testing from the heart and kidney transplant departments. I was waiting to hear from Dr. Hanna to tell me I was approved and that I was on the waiting list for a heart and kidney transplant. I also started to suffer from neuropathy in in my feet during 2021. In November 2020, I found out I had skin cancer. I went back eight times from November 2020 to September 2023 to remove cancerous cells from my hands, left ear, and left arm. The skin on my face and arms look terrible. I think I look like a lizard man.

At age thirty-three, I start to correspond with my future wife, Dr. Julia V. Knyaseva, who lived in Togliatti, Russia. We communicated by letters and phone calls for two years. By then I knew she was the one I wanted to marry. I arranged to visit her and her family in Russia by getting a visa and getting my passport. I had decided I would propose to her while visiting. I took her out to dinner and dancing. We got back to my hotel; I got on one knee and proposed to her. She accepted. We told her family and friends we were engaged. I asked a friend to help me arrange all the documents for fiancée visa so she could come and get married in the United States. I communicated through letters and phone calls while we waited on the fiancée visa.

A year later, I went back to visit and arrange the fiancée visa documents. In April 2002, she came to the States and met my family. We got married on August 3, 2002, and went on a two-week honeymoon. I also arranged for Julia's dad, Valeriy, and brother, Demetri, to come to the wedding. Valeriy and Demetri had issues on the day because of their airplane tickets. I had to contact my senator to help with them getting here. Julia's dad and brother spent the first week of our honeymoon in Las Vegas, Nevada, and then returned to Togliatti, Russia. The second week we spent at Myrtle Beach, South Carolina. We returned home to start our lives together.

Maria, our first child, was born on May 2004. Samuel, our second child, was born on March 2007. Aaron, our third child, was born on December 2011, and our fifth child was born on February 2015. Our fourth was never born. We got an abortion during a rough period, and to this day, we both regret it. I named our fourth child Joseph Ronald Devera if he was a boy and Janet Julia Devera if a girl. I will find out when I get to Heaven.

Around age forty-three in the year 2007, I was at a friend's house, David Preston. I made a comment, and he said, "God is going to give you a wake-up call."

I did not know how to reply to that statement, except I thought, *Right, yeah, sure.*

The following year, I got that wake-up call.

Afterlife Experience

My mom, Helen, took our two kids, Maria and Samuel, to her house in Parma, Ohio, the week before to celebrate Thanksgiving 2008. Two days before Thanksgiving 2008, my wife Julia and I were heading to my mom's house for Thanksgiving. We left our house around 6:00 p.m. on November 25, 2008. The drive took us about two and a half hours to get to my mom's house. We unloaded our luggage into the house and prepared to get ready for bed. As I was running up and down the stairs to our bedroom and bathroom, my chest started to hurt near my heart. I mentioned this to my wife Julia, and she said, "Let's go to the hospital now."

I said, "Let me see how I feel tomorrow. If I still feel bad, we will go to the Cleveland Clinic."

I woke up the next day and still was not feeling well, so my dad Richard and my wife took me to the Cleveland Clinic at Cleveland, Ohio. The Cleveland Clinic checked me in right away and performed electrocardiogram (EKG) to check on the heart attack status. I did not have a heart attack, so they got me into a room so they could schedule and perform heart angioplasty surgery the day after Thanksgiving, November 28, 2008. The doctors found three blockages they could not repair since the blockages were in very small arteries, and heart stent insertions would not work, so they told me they would perform open-heart surgery with possibly four or five bypasses. The doctors scheduled the open-heart surgery for December 3, 2008.

The doctor came to visit me in my room to explain the open-heart procedure to my wife and me. The doctor stated they would take arteries from my legs for the four or five bypasses. The arteries were attached to the heart in different locations around the heart to increase blood flow. I also talked to a lawyer supplied by Cleveland Clinic to create a last will and testament. This last will and testament gives you an idea how dangerous this operation can be and how nervous I was and how scared my wife was.

On December 3, 2008, the nurses came and got me from my room to prepare for the open-heart surgery. My mom, dad, brothers, and wife were waiting for me to be taken into surgery. My family said they would pray for me and wait for me to come out of surgery. I said I loved them and I would see them when I was done with surgery. I was a little scared not knowing what to expect with an eight-hour operation.

The nurses rolled me into surgery and put me on the operating table. The nurses gave me a drug to knock me out. I was counting backward from 100, 99, 98, and that was the last thing I remember.

My doctor told me later that they had performed four bypasses and cleaned out a lot of cholesterol buildup. As they were closing me up, I had heart fibrillation, and I died on the operating table. The doctors proceeded to open me up and shocked my heart directly three times to revive me. The doctors then found the issue—a leakage under the heart where they added another bypass. The eight-hour surgery turned out to be eighteen hours and multiple times back to surgery on different days.

The first time I woke up, I was in Hell. It was a dead forest as far as I could see, and there were thousands of demons as far as my eyes could see. The demons were different sizes—small and big—and some were misshapen or deformed. Some even looked human except for the eyes, claws, and horns on their heads. I also knew things, and I don't know how I knew these things, I just did, such as the black stuff in the trees, I knew if it touched me, I knew it would harm me. I also knew the demons were going to try and keep me here in Hell.

When I first woke up in Hell, I thought, *That's it, you screwed up*. Then I started to think, *Wait, I love Jesus, my wife, my two children, my mom and dad, and my friends*. Therefore, I started to pray. "Our Father, which art in heaven, hallowed be thy name. Thy kingdom come. Thy will be done on earth as it is in heaven. Please take away these demons so they do not harm others or me in Jesus's name. Amen."

I saw demons just disappear before my eyes, but there were so many demons, they kept coming after me. So I said the prayer again. "Our Father, which art in heaven, hallowed be thy name. Thy kingdom come. Thy will be done on earth as it is in heaven. Please take away these demons so they do not harm others or me in Jesus's name. Amen."

Again, demons disappeared. Then a human-looking demon came to me, sat next to me, and started to torture my hand. I had to direct the prayer directly at him for him to disappear. My right hand was hurt for a long time after, and the feeling eventually came back after a year. I felt I was there for many days until I could not stay awake much longer. I was very tired and fighting to stay awake because I knew if I fell asleep, they had me. I could not fight the sleepiness any longer.

I woke again, and this time, my first thoughts were the demons had taken me to my place of punishment. When I woke again in Hell, I was in a cave, and the demons were different looking. They looked like ghosts that you could see through, and the demons had the reddest eyes I had ever seen. These demons were male- and female-looking. The demons were floating above me. These demons were doing sexual acts with each other, and I knew they were going to do those sexual acts to me and keep me in Hell. I thought, *That's it, you screwed up*. Then I started to think, *Wait, I love Jesus, my wife, my two children, my mom and dad, and my friends*. Therefore, I started to pray again. "Our Father, which art in heaven, hallowed be thy name. Thy kingdom come. Thy will be done on earth as it is in heaven. Please take away these demons so they do not harm others or me in Jesus's name. Amen." These demons started to melt on top of my chest. I felt a lot of pain from this, so I prayed to God to take these demons away faster since they were hurting me in Jesus's name, and God did that for me. I said this prayer many times to get rid of the demons and black stuff in the cave also. The black stuff was similar to the black stuff in the trees.

A bright light eventually came into the cave, and I started to hear voices, which was the nurses and doctors working in the intensive care unit (ICU). I woke up after ten days in a coma. The doctors took me back to surgery three more times to help clean me out of more issues the doctors identified.

I believe I was saved because my family members and relatives put out a call to churches everywhere to pray to God to give Ronald Devera a second chance, and blessed am I for God heard and showed me mercy. I do not fear death anymore for Jesus walks with me.

CHAPTER 7

Awake

When I woke up in the intensive care unit (ICU) on December 13, 2008, I had all kinds of equipment and twenty tubes in me to keep me alive. I had breathing tubes, a feeding tube, and tubes to remove fluids and waste. The nurse told me my family members were here to see me. The nurse asked if I was okay to see them. I nodded yes to allow them to see me since I could not talk with the tubes in my mouth. When they came the first time, I went into convulsions since liquids got into my breathing tubes, and I started to choke. They made my family leave to help me get my breathing tubes cleared out. My family came back again to see me later, but only one at a time. My wife came first to see me, then my mom and then my dad. My wife told me later that she and my dad got into a car accident as he was taking her back home to go to work. The Saturn Vue was totaled.

I wanted to apologize to my dad Richard for the harm I caused between us while growing up and to others I know I hurt once I recovered from surgery and got a chance to visit them. I apologized to my dad through notes when he visited, and he said I did not need to, and I said yes, I did. We made peace with each other. I even forgave Renee, my long-forgotten girlfriend, who had hurt me a long time ago. I forgave my biological father also for leaving me as a child. I tried to reach Bob Russel and ask for his forgiveness, and I also forgave him for breaking our friendship.

The next day, December 14, 2008, I was taken out of ICU and taken to another area to be watched and to recover. While I was in recovery, I told my family through notes that I went to Hell, and I wanted to be baptized since I was never baptized. The doctors stated they could not allow this since I had all these tubes and equipment hooked up to my body. I said, "I don't care. Let's find a way we can get this done." My body was recovering very fast; I did not need any painkillers since I felt no pain. The nurse and doctor finally took the tube out of my mouth so I could talk a little. I had to eat ice and popsicles to soothe my throat from the feeding tube I had.

As time progressed, more tubes were removed from my body, and I was able to start walking around slowly. While walking one day, I ran into my doctor who performed the open-heart surgery. He introduced himself, and he said to me, "You should not be here. I did everything by the book, but somebody upstairs in Heaven likes you very much."

I said, "Yes, God loves me." Even the nurses were calling me the miracle child that year for 2008.

I prayed to God, asking him to get me out of the hospital so I could spend Christmas with my children at home. On December 18, 2008, I was released from the hospital. I asked my mom to arrange my baptism. My mom worked the baptism out with her pastor, and he agreed. Two people held me up while Pastor Bill baptized me. On December 22, 2008, I was baptized at my mom's church, and I told my afterlife experience to the congregation.

My uncle Alvin visited me in the hospital while I was recovering. He found out about my afterlife experience and wanted to tell me about my dad's afterlife experience before he passed away.

Ronald Lincoln, my dad, went into the hospital for chest pains and died on the operating table. During his death, angels had come to him and were kissing him before he came back. He recovered from this and went on to help family members with anything they needed him to fix. Two weeks later, he died of a heart attack. He is in heaven serving God the Father.

C H A P T E R   8

Wife Awakens

While recovering from my open-heart surgery at home, my wife had doubts about my afterlife experience. She stated the anesthesia made me see things, and it was a dream. I told Julia it was not a dream; what I saw was real for I felt things and knew where I was.

While watching television, a Christian program was on, and we started to watch it. They were telling stories of people's afterlife experiences in Heaven and Hell. One of the men came up and started to talk about his afterlife experience in Hell where everything was in a dead forest, and there were demons of different size—small and big—and some were misshapen or deformed. Some even looked human except for the eyes, claws, and horns on their heads.

I said to my wife Julia, "See, I told you it was true."

She had a look of surprise on her face. She believed me after that. She also had an experience that day that I died.

Julia was asking my brothers, Daryl and Keith, where Mom was at since she was afraid and wanted to be close to her. Keith and Daryl told her Mom went to the chapel to pray. Julia headed to the chapel to be with Mom. Mom was exiting the chapel, and Julia noticed a glow and peace around Mom. When she met up with her and touched her hands, she instantly felt a shock wave enter her entire body. Julia asked her what that was. Mom said it was the Holy Spirit,

19

and it told her Ronald was going to be okay. Julia spent the rest of day with Mom and felt at peace and was no longer afraid.

I had a dream of a cross that Jesus was crucified on, so I went to Home Depot and bought two four-by-eight pieces of wood. I made a three-foot-by-two-foot cross and another similar to it. One now hangs in my bedroom over my bed, and the other I gave to my mom. I was jealous since I did not get to see Jesus in my afterlife experience. Therefore, I had a dream of Jesus, who came to me, and I hugged him. I thought to myself, *Was that real?* The following night, I had the same dream. Jesus loves us so much, we cannot comprehend the love he feels for us.

Julia V. Knyazeva was born on November 11 and grew up in Togliatti, Union of Soviet Socialist Republics (USSR). Her parents are Valeriy Knyazev and Maria Knyazeva. Maria Knyazeva was a health inspector who passed away on May 2002. Valeriy Knyazev was a medical doctor at a hospital who passed away on March 2015.

After Julia and I were married, she told me her mom liked me. Julia's dad, Valeriy, I got to know over time and loved him like a dad. He took me to my first bathhouse in Russia. He also took me fishing on a river near Togliatti. I miss them both very much.

CHAPTER 9

I Know

I know Heaven exists, and God lives in me. I also know Hell and *satan* (not capitalized on purpose) exists. You must be baptized, ask God's forgiveness of all your sins, pray every day for your family, friends, and enemies, read your Bible to know God and your purpose, and forgive those who hurt you and those you have hurt. We must be humble in this life just as Jesus was humble. Did he not wash the disciples' feet at the last supper? Therefore, humble thyself before the Lord.

This world is a test of who you can be and where you will end up. I pray and hope it is Heaven. You do not want to go to Hell. I now live to serve the Father, Jesus, and Holy Spirit. Those tests shall be difficult, but are necessary so you can become the man or woman God wants you to become in this life so you can find God before your time on earth comes to an end. Even Job in the Bible was tested when satan came to God and asked to prove Job (Job 1–42, AKJV) was worthy of God's love and grace.

I have a family friend who I prayed for every day. I will call the mother Jackie, her daughter Janice, who is six years old, and her son David, who is five years old. Jackie was remarried to a man named Nick. Nick was a hardworking man who worked for a dealership as a car salesman. Nick even helped me buy a minivan for a good price when I needed a new vehicle.

When Janice was age sixteen, an angel spoke to her in a dream. "When are you going to stop this hurting and tell your mother?" The next morning, Janice told her mother that Nick had been molesting her for the last ten years. Jackie left in the middle of the night with her two kids to stay with a friend from work. She later moved in with my family as she was dealing with this nightmare.

The point of this story is to tell you the power of prayer. God sent an angel to give courage to Janice when she needed it most. Never stop praying for those around you.

CHAPTER 10

Transplants

The year is 2019, and my wife Julia and I went to the Cleveland Clinic in Florida. The Cleveland Clinic in Ohio recommended we go there to get a better chance to receive a heart and kidney transplant. We received a letter from Cleveland Clinic, Florida, stating we got approved on July 1, 2019.

On August 19, 2020, we arrived at my mom's house. The wife and I were in Parma, Ohio, to visit Cleveland Clinic for medical appointments I had on August 20, 2020. At 4:00 a.m. on August 20, 2020, we received a call from Cleveland Clinic, Florida, stating they had a heart and kidney available for transplant. "Do you want to receive it?" they asked me. I said yes, and we started to work on getting plane tickets for a 6:00 a.m. flight straight to the Cleveland Clinic in Florida. I called my cousin Scott for a ride to the airport. Scott picked us up at 5:25 a.m. from my mom's house in Parma, Ohio. We arrived at the Cleveland airport and unloaded my dialysis machine and dialysis fluids, medical gear, and luggage. We got our luggage checked in, and Spirit Airline charged fifty dollars for additional luggage. We got tickets and proceeded to go through security. We got to the terminal and sat down and waited for them to call us to board the plane.

The flight arrived in Florida at 10:00 a.m. on August 20, 2020. We retrieved our luggage at the Florida airport. The Cleveland

Clinic, Florida had an ambulance waiting at the airport to pick us up. The wife and I loaded in the ambulance, and the driver turned on sirens and proceeded to Cleveland Clinic, Florida. We arrived at the Cleveland Clinic and went straight to my room for check-in and to prepare for surgery. My doctors and surgery personnel came to see me and prepare me for surgery.

I told my wife I loved her and would see her when I woke up. It was a long wait for my wife. The surgery nurse eventually came for me and took me to surgery. The nurses and doctors put me on an operating table and prepared me with an IV line so the drug would knock me out for surgery. I was counting 100, 99, 98, 97, and that's the last thing I remember.

On August 19, 2020, I received my new heart. The operation took eleven hours. On August 20, 2020, I received my new kidney, and this operation took four hours. I was kept in a coma for two weeks so the surgeons could take me back to operating room for additional surgeries. I was taken back three additional times for cleaning of areas leaking body fluids and to ensure no issues were occurring. I was told later the doctors were happy with the new heart and new kidney transplants.

I was coming in and out of a drugged sleep as they eventually removed my feeding tube. I remember my wife Julia visiting me a couple of times, but I couldn't talk yet. I remember my mom talking to me on video calls a couple of times, but I still couldn't talk. I was very happy to see my wife and mom during those times, and I could only smile. I still don't know why I couldn't talk during those times. I wanted to but could not.

When I finally was awake on September 10, 2020, I was very alert and felt really good. My heart and kidney were functioning perfectly. I could not move my legs nor get up out of bed without assistance. They told me not to get up on my own as it was too risky. The physical therapy nurses would come help me get up and moving so I could start to walk around and exercise my legs and arm muscles. I would slowly walk to my therapy sessions and rest in a wheelchair when needed. I started to walk farther and farther.

I had this catheter in my privates, and I was telling the doctors and nurses there was a problem with the catheter, but no one listened to me. The urologist was in the hospital on September 15, 2020, next to my room and did not come to see me. And then he was supposed to come and see me on Tuesday, September 16, 2020, the next day but never showed up. I had the nurse call the urologist to me on Tuesday night since I was having an issue with the catheter. He refused to see me that night; instead, he would see me the following morning. The urologist showed up on Wednesday afternoon, and I told him we had to remove the catheter because of the issues I was feeling. He reluctantly agreed.

Infections

A few days later, I had my first issue of urinary tract infection (UTI). I had chills and a high fever, which is not good since I no longer have an immune system since it was being suppressed because of my new heart and new kidney. Your body considers new organs as foreign invaders, so your immune system will attack new organs. They put ice packs under my arms to lower my temperature of 102 degrees and got me on some antibiotic drugs to fight this infection. From September 2020 to February 2021, I was fighting this UTI infection.

I was scheduled to see the urologist on January 25, 2021, to see what was causing the UTI using a scope. The urologist said the infection was gone and that my bladder looked really good, except my prostate was slightly enlarged. I had to take medicine to shrink my prostate to normal. During the UTI infections and catching COVID-19, I became very angry with my doctors and was not understanding why God had forsaken me. I survived the COVID-19 virus; it took over a month, from November 2020 to December 2020, to recover. I caught COVID-19 a second time during May 2021. I did not feel sick at all during that time, but I did quarantine myself to ensure no one caught it. I learned later this was when God was closest to me. During the times we feel God is missing is when he is closest to us. We have to learn how to listen for him, which is not easy but possible.

On January 23, 2021, I was sick again. My lymph nodes were slightly swollen under my right armpit and very painful. I contacted the transplant team to inform them, and they said I should see my oncologist to see if it was my the non-Hodgkin's lymphoma. The nurse practitioner said, "This does not appear to be your cancer but some kind of infection."

They ordered a CT scan to be sure it was not the cancer. The CT scan confirmed it was not my cancer but some kind of infection. The heart transplant doctor ordered a blood test for infectious diseases. The left and right armpit were both infected, and I was experiencing severe pain. Based on the hospital scale, it was a 10. The Cleveland Clinic heart clinical lead told me to come to the hospital.

The wife took me up to Cleveland Clinic emergency to see the heart and kidney transplant teams on February 12, 2021. The doctors admitted me into hospital and started to run blood tests to see what type of infection I had in my skin. The infection was pseudomonas, a bacteria found within the skin. I was on multiple antibiotics to get rid of the infections within my two armpits.

I left the hospital on February 27, 2021. I completed my antibiotics on March 2, 2021. Thank you, Jesus—no more infections have occurred since my release from the hospital on February 27, 2021.

In March 2021, I was getting stronger, walking more, and doing weights to build muscle and strength. My one son Aaron got sick, and it spreads to my other son, wife, and mom. I was not feeling good; I was weak, and I was tired again. It felt like I was fighting something off, but not totally sick, thank you, Jesus. I was starting to get better on May 12, 2021. I started using weights and walking more, but it was taking longer to get my strength back.

In April 2021, I talked to heart and kidney doctors about my legs feeling heavy, numb, and not at full strength still after eight months after surgery. They tried a water pill for six days and worked on getting some of the swelling from my legs. I had also been seeing my wound care for my three toes on my left foot, an issue from the heart and kidney transplant for medication they had to use. The surgery caused blood flow loss to my feet, which caused them to become black. I had to keep pushing myself to walk more and more and keep using my weights so I can serve God the Father and my family as I was meant to do. I think my diabetes is interfering with my legs and feet. I like sweets, so I have to cut back and work on lowering my A1C.

CHAPTER 12

God's Blessing

On August 8, 2022, I was trying to finish writing my book. I had gained my strength back and suffered other difficulties financially, but God provided for my needs to replace two cars in accidents this year, one in January 9, 2022, and the second on May 16, 2022. Jesus was tempted during his life, and we as sinners will be tempted throughout our lives by satan to ensure we are worthy to enter the Kingdom of Heaven.

From October 2021 to August 2022, my wife Julia had many medical issues. Julia was recovering and getting back to work as a registered nurse (RN).

I did falter at times in my faith, but I did talk to God or read my Bible for my questions or issues to renew my faith. I learned that we must continue to pray for our family and others, attend a church of God, forgive those who have hurt us, tithe to our church and other worthy programs, read the Bible, and talk to God on a regular basis, especially when you have questions or don't understand things going on in your life.

I talked about a lot of issues in my life. I know there are many in this world who are suffering more than I have, but I know God has watched over and protected me as he does everyone else, whether they believe or not. We are God's children.

Prayers I Say

Dear Lord, your word says that I am to ask, and I shall receive, that my joy may be full right now, Lord. I thank you that my prayers are reaching Heaven, and when I pray, you are answering quickly. I decree that no hindering spirit can hinder or block my prayers in any way. In Jesus's name I pray. Amen.

Our Father, which art in Heaven, hallowed be thy name. Thy kingdom come. Thy will be done on earth as it is in Heaven. Give us this day our daily bread, and forgive us our debts as we forgive our debtors. And lead us not into temptation, but deliver us from evil. For thine is the kingdom, the power, and the glory forever. Amen.

Hail Mary, full of grace. Our Lord is with thee. Blessed art thou among women, and blessed is the fruit of thy womb, Jesus.

Holy Mary, Mother of God, pray for us sinners, now and at the hour of our death. Amen.

Glory be to the Father and the Son and the Holy Spirit, as it was in the beginning, is now and ever shall be, world without end. Amen.

Dear Jesus, today I claim health and healing in my body. The Bible says that by your stripes I was healed, and because of this covenant promise, the devil has no right to afflict or torment me physically. I claim a doctor confirmed manifestation of total healing from the crown of my head to the soles of my feet. I ask these in Jesus's name. Amen.

Our Mother, which art upon earth, hallowed be thy name. Thy kingdom come, and thy will be done in us as it is in thee. As thou sendest every day thy angels, send them to us also. Forgive us our sins, as we atone all our sins against thee. And lead us not into sickness, but deliver us from all evil, for thine is the earth, the body, and the health. Amen.

Heavenly Father, I believe that the wealth of the wicked is laid up for the just in the last days. Lord, I claim that I shall be too blessed to ever be depressed. I claim more than enough money to pay all my bills and to help everyone whom you lead me to as well. Lord, right now I claim more than a hundredfold on the offerings that I have given, and I take complete and total authority over the money the devil has fought me. In Jesus's name. Amen.

Dear Father, I love you, and I need you. Come into my heart, mind, body, and soul please. I ask these in Jesus's name. Amen.

Dear Father, Jesus, and Holy Spirit, I ask that your angels watch over (insert family names) throughout the day and night so no evil will touch or harm them forever, and may your angels guide and protect them. I ask these in Jesus's name. Amen.

Dear Father, Jesus, and Holy Spirit, I ask that your angels watch over (insert name) and (his wife's and children's names) so no evil will ever harm them and that angels will guide and protect them. I ask these in Jesus's name. Amen.

Dear Lord, I thank you for this day. I thank you for my being able to see and to hear this morning. I'm blessed because you are a forgiving God and an understanding God. You have done so much for me, and you keep on blessing me. Forgive me for every sin, past and present, I have done, said, or thought that was not pleasing to you. I ask now for your forgiveness. Please keep me safe from all danger and harm. Help me to start this day with a new attitude and plenty of gratitude. Let me make the best of each and every day to clear my mind so that I can hear from you. Please broaden my mind that I can accept all things. Let me not whine and whimper over things I have no control over. And give me the best response when I'm pushed beyond my limits. I know that when I can't pray, you listen to my heart. Continue to use me to do your will. Continue to bless me that I may be a blessing to others. Keep me strong that I may help the weak. Keep me uplifted that I may have words of encouragement for others. I pray for those who are lost and can't find their way. I pray for those who are misjudged and misunderstood. I pray for those who don't know you intimately. I pray for those that don't believe. But I thank you that I believe that God changes people and God changes things. I pray for all my sisters and brothers, for each and every family member in their households. I pray for peace, love, and joy in their homes; that they are out of debt and all their needs are met. I pray that every ear that hears this knows there is no problem, circumstance, or situation greater than God. Every battle is in your hands for you to fight. I pray that these words be received into the hearts of every ear that hears it in Jesus's name. Amen.

Dear Father,

I refuse to confess lack in 2023 for "my God shall supply all of my need according to His riches in glory by Christ Jesus" (Phil. 4:19).

I refuse to confess fear in 2023 for "God hath not given us the spirit of fear; but of power, and of love, and of a sound mind" (2 Tim. 1:7).

I refuse to confess defeat in 2023 for "God which always causeth us to triumph in Christ" (2 Cor. 2:14).

I refuse to confess that you can't in 2023 for "I can do all things through Christ who strengtheneth me" (Phil. 4:13).

I refuse to confess doubt or lack of faith in 2023 for "God hath dealt to every man the measure of faith" (Rom. 12:3).

I ask these in Jesus's name. Amen.

Dear Father, Jesus, and Holy Spirit, I ask that your angels watch over (insert name) so no evil will ever harm him/her, and the angels will guide him and protect him, and Father, I also ask that you find a good Christian wife/husband to love my brother/sister (insert name) and keep him/her on God's path. I ask these in Jesus name. Amen

Dear Father, Jesus, and Holy Spirit, I ask that your Angels watch over (Insert names) so no evil will ever harm them, and the angels will guide and protect them. I ask these in Jesus's name. Amen.

Dear Father, Jesus, and Holy Spirit, I ask that you stop these corporations, federal government, and the people involved from poisoning the world's food supply and killing and harming your children, Father, with genetically modified organisms (GMO). I ask these in Jesus's name. Amen.

Jesus, I come to you in faith right now. I decree that what I see going on around me is filtered through the Word of God and that all things are working together for my good. I also decree that 2023 shall be a year of health, healing, and prosperity. In your mighty name, Jesus, I pray. Amen.

God, you order the steps of a righteous person. If I have found favor in your eyes, guide every step I take and guide every action. Help me to recognize your path and discern where you want me to go. Open doors no one can shut, and shut every door I should avoid. Allow me to see clearly your direction without any confusion. Give me a clear sign today or this week regarding the direction I should take. I want to do your will. Guide me in Christ's name. Amen.

Lord, I realize that money is not everything, but it is necessary for the things I need. I want you trust me financially. Show me what I must do to become a great steward. Guide my steps so that my family and I can walk in your blessings and provisions. Help me to resist all the temptations that keep me from moving forward. I ask you to lead me in Christ's name. Amen.

Lord, my body is not responding as I hoped, but I recognize that you are the author and finisher of life. You knew me before I was born, and you formed every molecule of my genetic code. I ask you to heal me or guide me to the best solution. I hold on to your promise that says you work all things together for good. Your healing, your guidance, and your plan for my body in Christ's name, amen.

Lord, my family needs your help. We need your direction and guidance. I ask you to help me pass on your blessings to the generations that follow. Help us to serve you and become a family that walks in your provision and protection. Help us to lay aside our pride and eliminate competition so that we can experience your healing. Break the chains of generational dysfunction and set us free. I ask this in your precious name, Jesus, amen.

Dear Father, Jesus, and Holy Spirit, I pray that (insert children's names) will

1. Love the Lord their God with all their heart, soul, mind, and strength, and their neighbors as themselves.
2. Come to know Christ as Lord early in Life.
3. Develop a hatred for evil and sin.
4. Be protected from evil in each area of their lives spiritually, emotionally, mentally, and physically.
5. Be caught when they are guilty and receive the chastening of the Lord.
6. Receive wisdom, understanding, knowledge, and discretion from the Lord.
7. Respect and submit to those in authority.
8. Be surrounded by the right kinds of friends and avoid wrong friends.
9. Find a godly mate and raise godly children who will live for Christ.
10. Walk in sexual and moral purity throughout their lives.
11. Keep a clear conscience that remains tender before the Lord.
12. Not fear evil but walk in the fear of the Lord.
13. Be a blessing to your family, the church, and the cause of Christ in the world.
14. Be filled with the knowledge of God's will and be fruitful in every good work.
15. Overflow with love, discern what is best, and be blameless until the day of Christ.

I ask these in Jesus's name. Amen.

Dear Father, Jesus, and Holy Spirit, I pray that (insert wife's name), my wife, will

1. Love the Lord with all her heart, mind, soul, and strength.
2. Find her beauty and identity in Christ and reflect his character.
3. Love God's Word and allow it to bloom her into Christlikeness.
4. Be gracious, speaking the truth in love and avoiding gossip.
5. Respect me (insert husbands name), as her husband and submit to my leadership as unto the lord.
6. Be grateful and find her contentment in Christ, not her circumstances.
7. Be hospitable and diligently serve others with Christlike joy.
8. Bring her family good and not evil all the days of her life.
9. Have a godly older woman to mentor her and help her to grow.
10. Not believe lies that would devalue her role as a wife and mother.
11. Be loving, patient, hard to offend, and quick to forgive.
12. Have her sexual needs met only by me, her husband, and to meet my sexual needs.
13. Be devoted to prayer and effectively intercede for others.
14. Guide her home and children in a Christlike way.
15. Give no occasion for satan to accuse and reproach her.

I ask these in Jesus's name. Amen.

To him who is able to keep you from falling and to present you before his glorious presence without fault and with great joy. To the only God our Savior be glory, majesty, power, and authority, through Jesus Christ our Lord, before all ages, now and forever. I ask these in Jesus's name, amen.

Dear Father, please give me wisdom to understand, knowledge to do your plan, strength to keep moving forward, spiritual hearing to know you are speaking to me, and spiritual sight to see good and evil and power to glorify your name, Father. I ask these in Jesus's name. Amen.

Dear Father, hear my prayer for the United States of America. Please bring this country back to your glory, Father, as a godly nation now. Please bring godly, holy men and holy women to serve our country and protect it from the evil one and an ally to Jewish nations now. I ask blessings be bestowed upon the Jewish people so they may be faithful to our Father in Heaven. I ask these in Jesus's name. Amen.

Dear Father, Jesus, and Holy Spirit, hear my prayer for my (insert number) children. Please give them the knowledge, wisdom, strength, and understanding of all they need to succeed in school and this earthly world, which will prepare them for Heaven in Jesus's name. Amen.

Dear Father, Jesus, and Holy Spirit, hear my prayer for the people of earth and the countries they occupy. I ask in Jesus's name that world peace is given to all the people of earth so we may all serve Jesus Christ, our savior. Amen.

I pray that from his glorious, unlimited resources, he will give earth's people mighty inner strength through his Holy Spirit. And I pray that Christ will be more and more at home in earth's people's hearts as they trust in him. And may earth's people have power to understand how wide, how long, how high, and how deep his love really is. May earth's people experience the love of Christ…then they will be filled with the fullness of life and power that comes from God. I ask these in Jesus's name, amen.

Dear Father, Jesus, and Holy Spirit, I cancel mine and (insert wife's name)'s invitation to satan and his minions to do any more harm to us and our families. I ask these in Jesus's name. Amen.

Dear Father, Jesus, and Holy Spirit, I ask in Jesus's name that the following blessings are bestowed upon (insert family names), my family members:

1. Exaltation
2. Reproductiveness

3. Health
4. Prosperity
5. Victory
6. Authority
7. Above (Strength)
8. Wisdom
9. Communication

I ask these in Jesus's name. Amen.

Dear Father, Jesus, and Holy Spirit, please watch over (insert name), his wife (insert name), and their children so they will find your path you want them to follow and stay on, and may your angels guide and protect them. I ask this in Jesus's name. Amen.

Lord Jesus Christ, I believe that you are the son of God and the only way to God, that you died on the cross for my sins and rose again from the dead, and on the cross, you were made a curse with every curse that was due to me, that I might be redeemed from the curse and enter into the blessing. Lord, I confess any sins committed by me or by my ancestors. I ask for your forgiveness. I also forgive every other person who ever harmed or wronged me. I forgive them as I would have God forgive me. I also forgive myself. I renounce all contact with the occult in any form. I commit myself to get rid of any contact objects, and now, Lord, having received by faith your forgiveness, with authority I have as a child of God, I now release myself and those under my authority from any curse over our lives right now in the name of Jesus. I declare release, I claim it, and I receive it by faith in the name of Jesus. Thank you, Jesus. Thank you, Lord Jesus. Thank you.

Dear Father, Jesus, and Holy Spirit, I ask you to have your angels watch over my (insert number of children) children throughout the day and night and guide them so no evil or harm will ever come to them forever. I ask this in Jesus's name. Amen.

Dearest Jesus, I come to you today, thanking you for your promises of power in my life. Just as you promised Joshua and the children of Israel that the walls of Jericho would fall in seven days if they obeyed you and marched around them, so you have also made precious promises of power in your word to me. You have promised me in 1 Peter 2:24 that I am healed by your stripes, and I claim it. You have also promised me in Psalm 112:3 that there will be much wealth and riches in my house if I will fear you and delight in your commandments. I also claim your promises of prosperity. Lord, I know that you are a good God and that you will withhold no good thing from those who walk uprightly before you. Heavenly Father, if I have failed you or disappointed you in any way, please forgive me and show yourself strong on my behalf. I have determined to pray this prayer and expect miraculous intervention from you in my life in 2023. Hear my supplications and move for me miraculously as you have done so many times in the past. Thank you, Lord, in Jesus's holy name I pray. Amen.

He who reads this prayer, listens to it, or keeps it with him will never die of sudden death or drown, nor be struck by venom, nor fall into the hands of the enemy, nor be burned in any fire, nor surrender in battle. Pray this prayer for nine mornings for any intention.

O Saint Joseph, whose protection is so great, so strong, and so immediate before the throne of God, I entrust to you all my intentions and desires. Help me, Saint Joseph, with your powerful intercession to obtain all the spiritual blessings through the intercession of your adopted son, Jesus Christ our Lord, so that, entrusting me here on earth with your heavenly power, you tribute my thanks and homage. O Saint Joseph, I never tire of contemplating you with Jesus asleep in your arms. I dare not draw near as he rests with your heart. Embrace him in my name. Kiss his tender face for me and ask him to give me back this kiss when I breathe my last breath. Saint Joseph, patron of departed souls, pray for me! Amen.

O most Holy Heart of Jesus, the fountain of every blessing, I adore you, I love you, and with lively sorrow for my sins, I offer you this poor heart of mine. Make me humble, patient, pure, and wholly obedient to your will. Grant, Good Jesus, that I may live in you and for you. Protect me in the midst of danger. Comfort me in my afflictions. Give me health of body, assistance in my temporal needs, your blessings on all that I do, and the grace of a holy death. Amen.

O kindly Saint Raphael the Archangel, I invoke you as the patron of those who have been struck by disease or bodily infirmity. You have prepared the remedy that healed Tobias's blindness, and his name means "the Lord heals." I turn to you, begging your divine assistance in my present need: to (insert what do you need healed). If it be of God's will, cure my illnesses, or at least grant me the grace and strength I need to endure it patiently, offering it for the forgiveness of my sins and for the salvation of my soul. Teach me to unite my sufferings with those of Jesus and Mary and to seek the grace of God in prayer and communion. I want to imitate you in your eagerness to do God's will in all things. Like young Tobias, I choose you as my companion on my journey through this valley of tears. I want to follow your inspirations every step of the way so that I can reach the end of my journey under your constant protection and in the grace of God. Archangel Saint Raphael, you revealed yourself as the divine assistant of the throne of God. Come into my life and help me in this moment of trial. Grant me the grace and blessing of God and the favor I ask of you for your powerful intercession. Great physician of God, heal me as thou didst with Tobias, if this be the will of the Creator. Saint Raphael, resource of God, angel of health, medicine of God, pray for me. Amen.

Lord Almighty, into your hands I give my soul and my body. Oh Lord Jesus! Grant me strength to bear the cross as yourself. Teach me to bear it with great humility, that the Blessed Virgin may fill me with the Holy Spirit. Preserve my soul and lead it to life everlasting. Amen.

Whoever reads or wears it on him will never burn or drown, nor will any poison have effect on him. He will never be a prisoner of war, nor will he ever be vanquished. When a woman has labor pains, let her wear this prayer, and she will immediately be delivered. And when the child is born, let her place this prayer on the right side of the child, and he will be safely preserved from all accidents.

Whoever carries this prayer with him will never have any epileptic attacks, and if you see anyone having fits, place the prayer on his right side, and he will be cured immediately. "Whoever writes this prayer for himself or for others I will bless, but whoever scoffs and laughs at it will be doomed," says the Lord. When this prayer is in the house, the house will be safely guarded against thunder and lightning. Whoever reads this prayer daily will be warned three days before his death by a holy sign of the cross.

Let us pray the Holy Cross Prayer of the Lord Jesus Christ. Amen.

God's peace be to this home and to all who dwell within. You, O Lord, are the beginning and the end, the alpha and omega, carefully watching over us from birth until death. Bless this door of our house, and in your goodness, send your holy angel from Heaven to watch over and protect us, to be with us and give us comfort and encouragement. As we pass through this door, draw us more deeply into your presence, and may a spirit of humility, goodness, mildness, and gratitude prevail here.

O Lord, you are the door to eternal life. Bless our entrances and exits from this home and pour out on us heavenly dew in good measure as well as an abundance of earthly needs. At our lowly coming, be pleased to bless and sanctify this home, as you once were pleased to bless the home of Abraham, Isaac, and Jacob. Within these walls, let your angels of light preside and stand watch over those who live here. May this blessing remain on this place and on us who live here now and always. Amen.

Photos

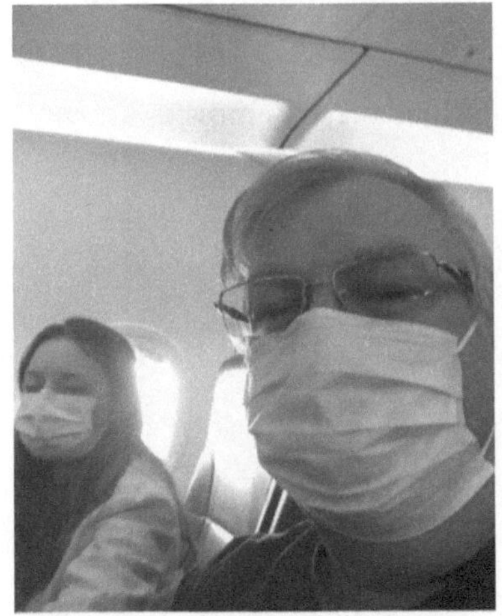

Plane to Florida Transplants

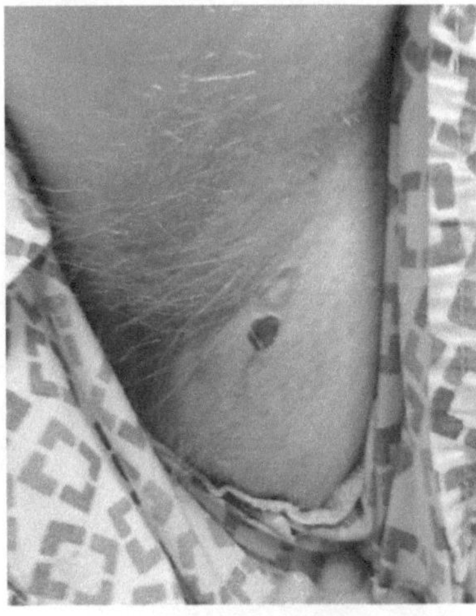

Biopsy for Underarm

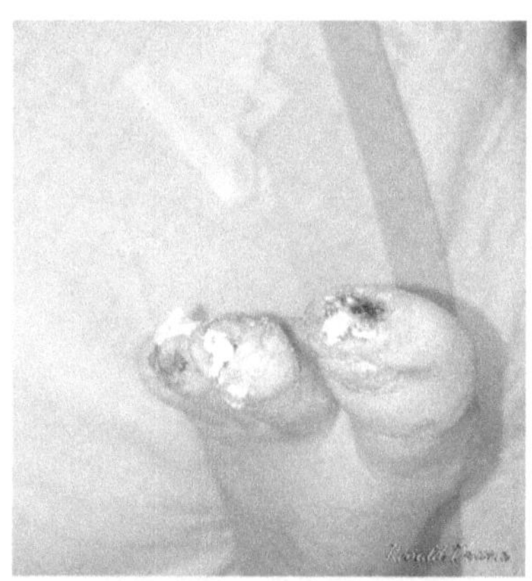

Medicine Caused This
on Foot from Surgery

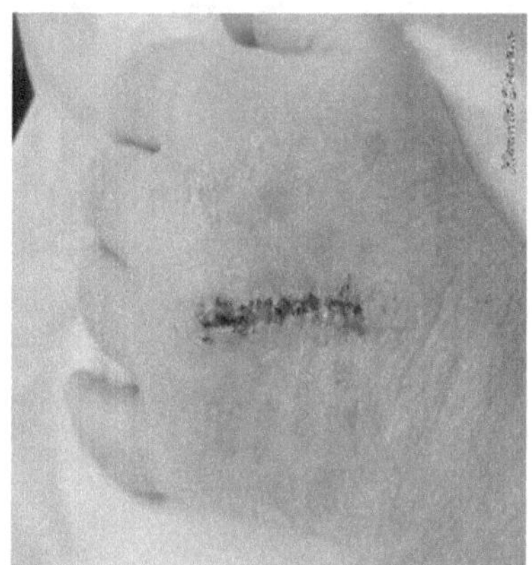

Skin Cancer Removed

Skin Cancer

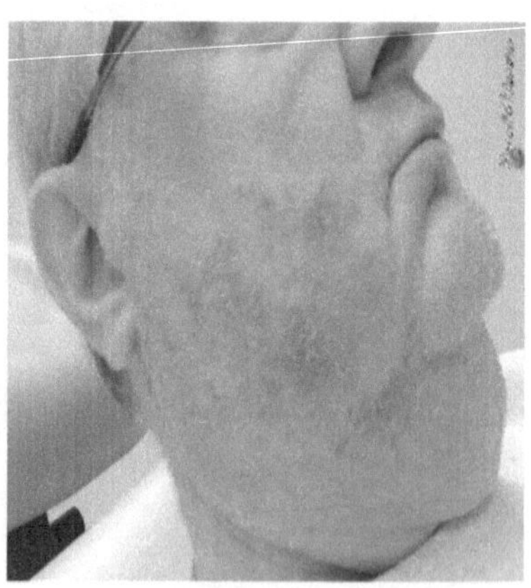

Skin Cancer

43

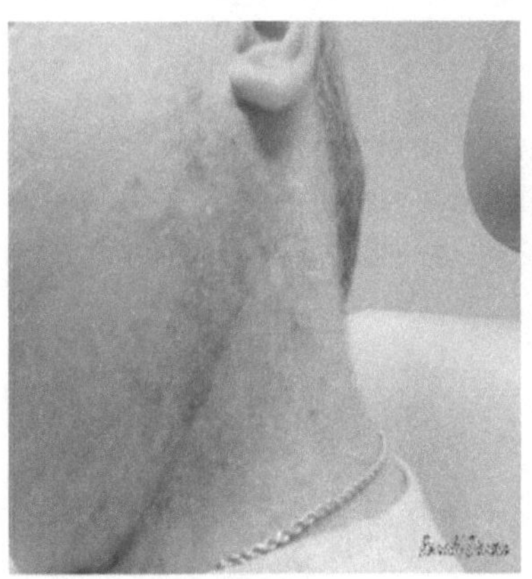

Skin Cancer

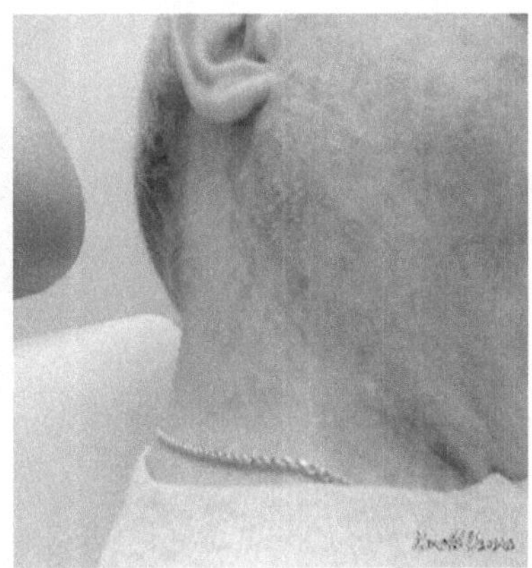

Skin Cancer

ABOUT THE AUTHOR

Ronald Devera was born in Cleveland, Ohio, on July 1964. He was raised as a Christian but did not truly follow Jesus Christ as we should follow him. He knew God as a young child, but lost it through sins that he committed.

He has been married for twenty-one years and has four children and another that he and his wife support with gifts.